Genealogy Journal
My Ancestral Family Tree

All rights reserved. No part of this book may be copied or reproduced by any means, whether electronic or mechanical. You cannot photocopy, record or transmit any material in the book without express written consent from the author.

Compiled and Designed by: Quinthos Publishing

Copyright 2020

Edition: 1

ISBN: 9798664969115

This journal belongs to:

_____

Contents

Introduction	6
Researching Your Family History	7
10 Quick Tips	10
Me – Researcher's Details	13
Family Tree	14
Father & Mother	16
Grandparents – Paternal Line	17
Great Grandparents – Paternal Line	18
Great Grandparents – Paternal Line	19
Great Great Grandparents – Paternal Line	20
Great Great Grandparents – Paternal Line	21
Great Great Grandparents – Paternal Line	22
Great Great Grandparents – Paternal Line	23
Great Great Great Grandparents – Paternal Line	24
Great Great Great Grandparents – Paternal Line	25
Great Great Great Grandparents – Paternal Line	26
Great Great Great Grandparents – Paternal Line	27
Great Great Great Grandparents – Paternal Line	28
Great Great Great Grandparents – Paternal Line	29
Great Great Great Grandparents – Paternal Line	30
Great Great Great Grandparents – Paternal Line	31
Maternal Line	32
Grandparents – Maternal Line	33
Great Grandparents – Maternal Line	34
Great Grandparents – Maternal Line	35
Great Great Grandparents – Maternal Line	36
Great Great Grandparents – Maternal Line	37
Great Great Grandparents – Maternal Line	38
Great Great Grandparents – Maternal Line	39
Great Great Great Grandparents – Maternal Line	40
Great Great Great Grandparents – Maternal Line	41
Great Great Great Grandparents – Maternal Line	42
Great Great Great Grandparents – Maternal Line	43
Great Great Great Grandparents – Maternal Line	44
Great Great Great Grandparents – Maternal Line	45
Great Great Great Grandparents – Maternal Line	46
Great Great Great Grandparents – Maternal Line	47
Certificates Log	48
Ancestors' Military Information	52
Female Ancestors in World War I & II	53
Ancestors who Emigrated	54
Ancestors' Grave Information	55
Family Stories and Legends to Uncover	56
Photographs	57
Additional Children	64
Additional Family Trees	66
Helpful Websites	72
Notes	73
Research Log	81

Introduction

This genealogy journal has been created to help you log at least six generations of your family, on both your paternal (father) and maternal (mother) sides. These include family tree templates to help you to plot your relatives in a clear, visual and understandable way over a double-page spread, along with forms for each ancestor detailing their names, occupations, place of birth, marriages, death and issue (children). The first sixteen pages of the family record detail the paternal side of your family (the left side of the family tree), followed by a further fifteen pages detailing the maternal side of your family (the right side of your family tree). There is also an additional set of blank family tree templates at the back of the book so that you can add further generations or record a particular family in further detail if you wish.

Included in this journal are a number of guides and recommendations to assist you on your genealogical journey, along with advice, directions and several handy data logs for information such as military information, emigration details, burial and memorial information, family legends, a photographs section and additional resources and overflow records, plus a list of useful websites that you may wish you use or consult. In addition, you will find a certificates log to tick-off and complete each time you source a birth, death or marriage certificate, as well as a resource log to help you to reference sources in case you need to revisit them in the future.

Everything has been designed to aid your research and keep your information simple and organised, along with a 'notes' section at the back of the book, where you can scribble information as you find it so that all of your notes, breakthroughs and questions can be kept together in one place.

Start your journey by reading the advice and tips over the next few pages, then complete the first form all about you, including details on your birth, occupation, children, achievements and anything else you would like to be known about you (page 13). From there you can begin your family tree research, using the tree template to plot your parents first, then grandparents, and any other ancestors that you are certain of.

In your family tree (on pages 14 and 15), each box refers to a page number where you can write about your ancestor in further detail. Make sure that you complete the correct information on the correct page so that it correlates with the corresponding box on your family tree. *For example, on page 15 (your mother's side of the family) the boxes that refer to your mother's parents (your maternal grandparents) have p33 next to them, this means that you need to go to page 33 to fill in more detailed information about those ancestors.*

If you have obtained certificates of an ancestor's birth, marriage or death, don't forget to tick them off in the Certificates Log.

Good luck on your ancestral journey.

Researching Your Family History

Tracing your ancestral lineage can be a complex and time-consuming undertaking but by taking some simple steps, following these tips and utilizing the resources in this book, your journey should be much easier.

1. Start With What You Know

Though it can be tempting to launch into your quest straight away by researching unknown ancestors or seeking to draw up your family tree, starting with a clear and stable foundation is the best method to make your future research easier. Start by gathering together all the information you already have about your family, beginning with yourself and any siblings, then your parents, aunts, uncles and cousins etc. Note down birth dates, marriages, deaths, places they have lived, occupations, places they worked, service information and so on until you have compiled a thorough record of the relatives you *do* know.

Keep A Notebook – it is essential that you log any information you come across as you gather it. It is easy to lose track of details or misremember information and the practice of writing it down will save you time and effort later on. Allot a double page per each couple, for example grandfather's information on one page and grandmother's information on the facing page. This will allow you to make sense of information gathered. When you have evidence that the information you have is correct, you can then write the information into this journal.

2. Ask Relatives

Even if you think you have remembered everything there is to know about your family, relatives might remember small details you may have missed through age, time or even a different perspective. Ask questions, get them thinking and note down any information they may recall about other family members. Sit down with them and carry out an interview regarding events, marriages, holidays and childhood stories – recalling memories often recovers forgotten information, and you may find out interesting information you didn't know before, such as people's character or achievements.

3. Graves

Headstones often hold a lot of information such as names, dates, ages, regimental details and even trade markings; therefore visiting the graves of deceased relatives may provide that extra clue to help move your research forward.

Websites such as *FindMyGrave.com* or local authority websites are often useful tools to help you locate lost or unknown graves.

4. Certificates

Birth, death and marriage certificates hold a wealth of information to support your research and aid your search. Read them carefully and note down each section – this will ensure you do not overlook a vital snippet of information. By obtaining certificates of your closest ancestors you will gain the necessary information required to move back another generation, step-by-step, through each ancestral line. You can obtain copies of certificates via the registry offices in the area where your ancestor was born or lived at the time or their marriage or death (these are where births, deaths and marriages are registered). Some family-search websites also offer a service (at a cost) to obtain certificates on your behalf.

5. Genealogy Websites

Family search websites hold extensive information and they are invaluable when researching your family tree, particularly as many now hold decades' worth of census records, providing crucial information about your ancestor's living conditions, fellow lodgers and occupations. Some offer their service for free while others charge varying amounts. However, many libraries offer access to these website for free

Extending Your Search

Once you have gathered information from birth, marriage and death certificates and census records, you may want to carry out more in-depth research by finding out more about individual ancestors or about extended family members (such as brothers and sisters of your great grandparents). There are many records to help you with your search such as street directories, which list whole families living at each address. There are also school and education records (extended family often went to the same school), electoral registers, rates records, court records, workhouse records, passage lists (from international travel), immigration records, hospital lists, and so on. Each county (and cities) have their own archives that you may access online or via a county record office. The list of websites provided in this book will prove to be a useful starting point.

i. Directories, Diaries and Documents

If you find yourself stuck in your research try to think a little outside the box, there are numerous places where additional information can be found, such as:
   a. Parish and Church Records: Each church, up until 1837, kept records of baptisms, marriages and burials. Parish records can normally be found at the church itself, at the local county record office or even online on websites such as *ParishRegister.co.uk*
   b. Trade Directories and Guilds: You can often find out the occupation of individuals in census records, once you have this information you can consult any number of trade directory books and websites to assist your research further. There are websites that focus specifically on individual occupations, such as blacksmiths, engineers and doctors, as well as online resources that hold various directories such as *SpecialCollections.le.ac.uk*, the national archives and [in the UK] in the City and County Directories (from 1600s to 1900s). A list of useful websites can be found within this book.
   c. War Records and Diaries: The National Archives provide access to 1.5 million war diaries from various conflicts and wars. *GreatWar.co.uk* and *Forces-War-Records.co.uk/Records* may help you find your ancestors' service information. Many of these websites charge users to use their services so making use of free trial periods may be particularly useful.

ii. Newspapers and Journals

Historical publications can hold a wealth of information on local stories or events that may refer to your ancestors. There are both paper archives and digital archives covering sporting events, probates and wills, news and events. The main library in your town or city often house newspapers on microfilm that you can access to read through. Online archives include *BritishNewspaperArchive.co.uk* and *NewspaperArchives.com* where you can click through to find the particular nation's newspapers you're looking for.

iii. Ordnance Survey Maps

These maps cover areas of Great Britain over the past two hundred years giving insight into the area your ancestor lived and worked during the time they were alive. They show roads, farmland, and industrial areas in great detail, as well as place names, topographical features and much more. OS maps can be purchased online and at various bookstores. Visiting the areas where your ancestors once lived can also be inspiring. If you can access registry offices, local churches (for parish records) and graveyards in the area they lived it can also be very rewarding in terms of information gathering.

iv. DNA Testing

Testing can 'estimate' your origins to more than 500 regions around the world. It also enables you to connect with (via ancestry search websites) and cross-reference your ancestral origins with other peoples' records that may have also taken a test and are distantly (or closely) related to you and/or your ancestor. Read up on different DNA tests before choosing which to take, some tests may be more suitable for what you're looking for, for examples autosomal DNA tests trace both your maternal *and* paternal lineage while many just test your paternal side. These test can offer a host of unexpected clues as they not only read your DNA, and that which you share with your parents but also the 25% of DNA from your grandparents and 12.5% DNA you share with great-grandparents and so on.

v. Help

When you get stuck or feel you could benefit from some extra help there are numerous places to turn. A family history help desk can be found at many libraries and county record offices. Look for local family history societies via the Federation of Family History Societies (*FFHS.org.uk*). There are also professional genealogists who you can pay to search on your behalf. Many family history search websites also have forums and blogs where fellow researches offer support and advice.

Note: Remember to consider privacy. Check your privacy settings when you sign up with search websites, by using these services you may be allowing companies the right to your data, make sure to check their policy and assess what you feel safe/comfortable doing.

10 Quick Tips

1. Use a pencil when completing your notes and records. It is much easier to erase incorrect information and start again. Use ink only when you have definitive evidence.

2. Keep to your notebook or research book. It can be tempting to scribble some quick information on some handy notepaper, but this very often leads to confusion. Keeping everything in one place makes the process much simpler. There are several note pages at the back of this book for any information you want to keep close to hand.

3. Plan ahead:
a) Who or what are you searching for next?
b) When searching use the 'Research Log' at the rear of this book to record where you searched and what information you found there. This prevents repetition and searching the same place twice, ultimately aiding future searches.
c) Don't get distracted. When some unexpected information appears during your search make a note to return to the information another time and keep to your planned search.
d) Focus on primary sources such as birth, death, marriage and census records. These, generally, hold the most accurate information and will assist you in moving forward with your research.

4. Be mindful of illiterate ancestors. Marriage certificates may offer a clue to whether your ancestor was literate. Illiterate people were often unable to write their own names and instead would mark their signature with a 'X'. This often meant that census details will have been written down for them either by a minister or clerk and, as such, may have misheard or misspelt family names i.e. Instead of 'Burk' the name may have been written down as 'Birk' or 'Berk' – this could affect your research going forward as you would need to consult both versions on the names to discover further ancestors.

5. It was commonplace for people to record their chosen name or nickname when completing forms such as a birth certificate. Therefore, though their given name may have been James they may have been known as (and therefore written down as) Jim, Jimmy or even Jack, for example. Many family history search websites provide an advanced search option known as the 'wildcard' where the system will also lookup known variants of a name. Look for the 'tips' or 'help' tabs on the website for information on how to use these 'wildcards'.

6. Though legal documents are official, they do not always record the truth. Be aware of misinformation. A male ancestor, for example, may record himself as a widow but he may have, in fact, been a bigamist by marrying for a second time when divorce was not an option. You may come across this when the information you have doesn't appear to make sense. The first wife may still be alive despite her husband being written down as a 'widow'.

7. If you suddenly can no longer find an ancestor in census records it may not, necessarily, mean that they have died. If your ancestor is not at an expected address, they may be at a temporary address somewhere else on the day that the census was taken. Search extended family, the local hospital's list, prison records, workhouse records, lodgings or public houses, even neighbours homes. If children cannot be found at their parents' address this may mean that they are visiting or living with relatives, or even living with a neighbour as a 'lodger' or 'adopted'. It was not uncommon for a child to be fostered temporarily (or longer) while family members worked away, were in hospital or suffering hardship. You may find the family reunited in the next census. Remember it was also not uncommon for children as young as nine to be living 'in service' as a servant.

8. Trial various family history search sites before you commit to one, do not just sign up with one because you have heard of it. There are many available, some of which can offer basic information for free. Do a little research first: What do they offer? How much do they cost? Are they easy to use? Do they offer a free trial?

9. Computers can be unreliable, so get into the habit of backing up any research you keep on your computer, such as digital archives you may have saved to your hard drive. Back up information on external devices too such as USBs, external hard drives, 'The Cloud' etc.

10. Do not give up! It is normal to have difficult search sessions or whole days/weeks without a breakthrough but don't give in. When you finally find that elusive piece of information you will experience a great sense of achievement. Finding another piece of your family history jigsaw feels very rewarding and may be invaluable to other researchers or relatives who may wish to learn about the tree in future.

Me

Name:	
Date of Birth:	Place of Birth:
Religion/Beliefs:	*(If applicable)* Baptism place/date:
Occupation:	Place of Residence:
Qualifications:	
Accomplishments:	
Community role/s:	
Other Information:	

Marriage/Civil Partnership

Date of Union:	Place of Union:
Witness 1:	Witness 2:
Name of Spouse:	Occupation of Spouse:
Birth Date of Spouse:	Spouse's Place of Birth:
Mother of Spouse:	Father of Spouse:
(If applicable) Surname upon Union:	

Children

Name:	Birth Date:	Occupation:	Name of Spouse:	Date of Union:	Other Information:

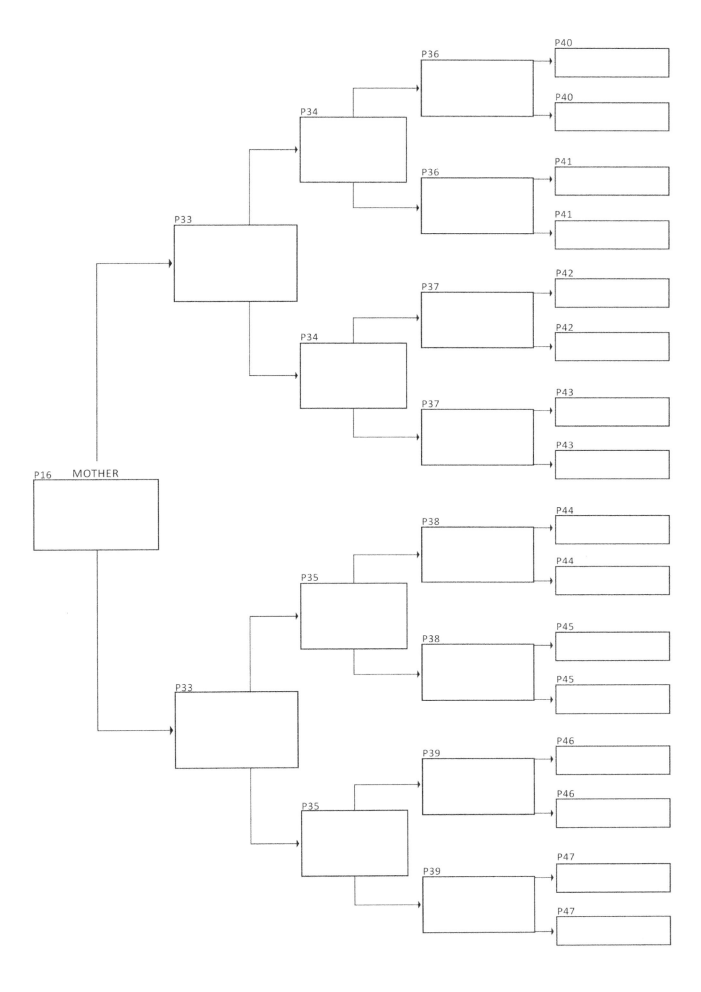

Father & Mother

Father		Mother	
Name:		Name:	
Date of Birth:	Place of Birth:	Date of Birth:	Place of Birth:
Baptised:		Baptised:	
Date of Death:	Place Buried: Grave Number:	Date of Death:	Place Buried: Grave Number:

Marriage Details

Date of Marriage:	Place of Marriage:	Witness 1:	Witness 2:
Groom's Name:	Age:	Occupation:	Additional Details:
Address:			
Father's Name:	Father's Occupation:		
Mother's Name:	Mother's Occupation:		
Bride's Name:	Age:	Occupation:	
Address:			
Father's Name:	Father's Occupation:		
Mother's Name:	Mother's Occupation:		

Children

Name:	Birth:	Death:	Occupation:	Marriage:	Spouse:	Information:

Census Information

Year:	Address:	Family / Details:	

Grandparents – *Paternal/Father's side*

Grandfather

Name:		Name (Grandmother):	
Date of Birth:	Place of Birth:	Date of Birth:	Place of Birth:
Baptised:		Baptised:	
Date of Death:	Place Buried: / Grave Number:	Date of Death:	Place Buried: / Grave Number:

Marriage Details

Date of Marriage:	Place of Marriage:	Witness 1:	Witness 2:
Groom's Name:	Age:	Occupation:	Additional Details:
Address:			
Father's Name:	Father's Occupation:		
Mother's Name:	Mother's Occupation:		
Bride's Name:	Age:	Occupation:	
Address:			
Father's Name:	Father's Occupation:		
Mother's Name:	Mother's Occupation:		

Children

Name:	Birth:	Death:	Occupation:	Marriage:	Spouse:	Information:

Census Information

Year:	Address:	Family / Details:	

Great Grandparents

Great Grandfather		Great Grandmother	
Name:		Name:	
Date of Birth:	Place of Birth:	Date of Birth:	Place of Birth:
Baptised:		Baptised:	
Date of Death:	Place Buried: Grave Number:	Date of Death:	Place Buried: Grave Number:

Marriage Details

Date of Marriage:	Place of Marriage:	Witness 1:	Witness 2:
Groom's Name:	Age:	Occupation:	Additional Details:
Address:			
Father's Name:	Father's Occupation:		
Mother's Name:	Mother's Occupation:		
Bride's Name:	Age:	Occupation:	
Address:			
Father's Name:	Father's Occupation:		
Mother's Name:	Mother's Occupation:		

Children

Name:	Birth:	Death:	Occupation:	Marriage:	Spouse:	Information:

Census Information

Year:	Address:	Family / Details:	

Great Grandparents

Great Grandfather		Great Grandmother	
Name:		Name:	
Date of Birth:	Place of Birth:	Date of Birth:	Place of Birth:
Baptised:		Baptised:	
Date of Death:	Place Buried: Grave Number:	Date of Death:	Place Buried: Grave Number:

Marriage Details

Date of Marriage:	Place of Marriage:	Witness 1:	Witness 2:
Groom's Name:	Age:	Occupation:	Additional Details:
Address:			
Father's Name:	Father's Occupation:		
Mother's Name:	Mother's Occupation:		
Bride's Name:	Age:	Occupation:	
Address:			
Father's Name:	Father's Occupation:		
Mother's Name:	Mother's Occupation:		

Children

Name:	Birth:	Death:	Occupation:	Marriage:	Spouse:	Information:

Census Information

Year:	Address:	Family / Details:	

Great Great Grandparents

x2 Great Grandfather		x2 Great Grandmother	
Name:		Name:	
Date of Birth:	Place of Birth:	Date of Birth:	Place of Birth:
Baptised:		Baptised:	
Date of Death:	Place Buried: Grave Number:	Date of Death:	Place Buried: Grave Number:

Marriage Details

Date of Marriage:	Place of Marriage:	Witness 1:	Witness 2:
Groom's Name:	Age:	Occupation:	Additional Details:
Address:			
Father's Name:	Father's Occupation:		
Mother's Name:	Mother's Occupation:		
Bride's Name:	Age:	Occupation:	
Address:			
Father's Name:	Father's Occupation:		
Mother's Name:	Mother's Occupation:		

Children

Name:	Birth:	Death:	Occupation:	Marriage:	Spouse:	Information:

Census Information

Year:	Address:	Family / Details:	

Great Great Grandparents

x2 Great Grandfather		x2 Great Grandmother	
Name:		Name:	
Date of Birth:	Place of Birth:	Date of Birth:	Place of Birth:
Baptised:		Baptised:	
Date of Death:	Place Buried: Grave Number:	Date of Death:	Place Buried: Grave Number:

Marriage Details

Date of Marriage:	Place of Marriage:	Witness 1:	Witness 2:
Groom's Name:	Age:	Occupation:	Additional Details:
Address:			
Father's Name:	Father's Occupation:		
Mother's Name:	Mother's Occupation:		
Bride's Name:	Age:	Occupation:	
Address:			
Father's Name:	Father's Occupation:		
Mother's Name:	Mother's Occupation:		

Children

Name:	Birth:	Death:	Occupation:	Marriage:	Spouse:	Information:

Census Information

Year:	Address:	Family / Details:	

Great Great Grandparents

x2 Great Grandfather		x2 Great Grandmother	
Name:		Name:	
Date of Birth:	Place of Birth:	Date of Birth:	Place of Birth:
Baptised:		Baptised:	
Date of Death:	Place Buried: Grave Number:	Date of Death:	Place Buried: Grave Number:

Marriage Details

Date of Marriage:	Place of Marriage:	Witness 1:	Witness 2:
Groom's Name:	Age:	Occupation:	Additional Details:
Address:			
Father's Name:	Father's Occupation:		
Mother's Name:	Mother's Occupation:		
Bride's Name:	Age:	Occupation:	
Address:			
Father's Name:	Father's Occupation:		
Mother's Name:	Mother's Occupation:		

Children

Name:	Birth:	Death:	Occupation:	Marriage:	Spouse:	Information:

Census Information

Year:	Address:	Family / Details:	

Great Great Grandparents

x2 Great Grandfather		x2 Great Grandmother	
Name:		Name:	
Date of Birth:	Place of Birth:	Date of Birth:	Place of Birth:
Baptised:		Baptised:	
Date of Death:	Place Buried: Grave Number:	Date of Death:	Place Buried: Grave Number:

Marriage Details

Date of Marriage:	Place of Marriage:	Witness 1:	Witness 2:
Groom's Name:	Age:	Occupation:	Additional Details:
Address:			
Father's Name:	Father's Occupation:		
Mother's Name:	Mother's Occupation:		
Bride's Name:	Age:	Occupation:	
Address:			
Father's Name:	Father's Occupation:		
Mother's Name:	Mother's Occupation:		

Children

Name:	Birth:	Death:	Occupation:	Marriage:	Spouse:	Information:

Census Information

Year:	Address:	Family / Details:	

Great Great Great Grandparents

x3 Great Grandfather		x3 Great Grandmother	
Name:		Name:	
Date of Birth:	Place of Birth:	Date of Birth:	Place of Birth:
Baptised:		Baptised:	
Date of Death:	Place Buried: Grave Number:	Date of Death:	Place Buried: Grave Number:

Marriage Details

Date of Marriage:	Place of Marriage:	Witness 1:	Witness 2:
Groom's Name:	Age:	Occupation:	Additional Details:
Address:			
Father's Name:	Father's Occupation:		
Mother's Name:	Mother's Occupation:		
Bride's Name:	Age:	Occupation:	
Address:			
Father's Name:	Father's Occupation:		
Mother's Name:	Mother's Occupation:		

Children

Name:	Birth:	Death:	Occupation:	Marriage:	Spouse:	Information:

Census Information

Year:	Address:	Family / Details:	

Great Great Great Grandparents

x3 Great Grandfather		x3 Great Grandmother	
Name:		Name:	
Date of Birth:	Place of Birth:	Date of Birth:	Place of Birth:
Baptised:		Baptised:	
Date of Death:	Place Buried: Grave Number:	Date of Death:	Place Buried: Grave Number:

Marriage Details

Date of Marriage:	Place of Marriage:	Witness 1:	Witness 2:
Groom's Name:	Age:	Occupation:	Additional Details:
Address:			
Father's Name:	Father's Occupation:		
Mother's Name:	Mother's Occupation:		
Bride's Name:	Age:	Occupation:	
Address:			
Father's Name:	Father's Occupation:		
Mother's Name:	Mother's Occupation:		

Children

Name:	Birth:	Death:	Occupation:	Marriage:	Spouse:	Information:

Census Information

Year:	Address:	Family / Details:	

Great Great Great Grandparents

x3 Great Grandfather		x3 Great Grandmother	
Name:		Name:	
Date of Birth:	Place of Birth:	Date of Birth:	Place of Birth:
Baptised:		Baptised:	
Date of Death:	Place Buried: Grave Number:	Date of Death:	Place Buried: Grave Number:

Marriage Details

Date of Marriage:	Place of Marriage:	Witness 1:	Witness 2:
Groom's Name:	Age:	Occupation:	Additional Details:
Address:			
Father's Name:	Father's Occupation:		
Mother's Name:	Mother's Occupation:		
Bride's Name:	Age:	Occupation:	
Address:			
Father's Name:	Father's Occupation:		
Mother's Name:	Mother's Occupation:		

Children

Name:	Birth:	Death:	Occupation:	Marriage:	Spouse:	Information:

Census Information

Year:	Address:	Family / Details:	

Great Great Great Grandparents

x3 Great Grandfather		x3 Great Grandmother	
Name:		Name:	
Date of Birth:	Place of Birth:	Date of Birth:	Place of Birth:
Baptised:		Baptised:	
Date of Death:	Place Buried: Grave Number:	Date of Death:	Place Buried: Grave Number:

Marriage Details

Date of Marriage:	Place of Marriage:	Witness 1:	Witness 2:
Groom's Name:	Age:	Occupation:	Additional Details:
Address:			
Father's Name:	Father's Occupation:		
Mother's Name:	Mother's Occupation:		
Bride's Name:	Age:	Occupation:	
Address:			
Father's Name:	Father's Occupation:		
Mother's Name:	Mother's Occupation:		

Children

Name:	Birth:	Death:	Occupation:	Marriage:	Spouse:	Information:

Census Information

Year:	Address:	Family / Details:	

Great Great Great Grandparents

x3 Great Grandfather		x3 Great Grandmother	
Name:		Name:	
Date of Birth:	Place of Birth:	Date of Birth:	Place of Birth:
Baptised:		Baptised:	
Date of Death:	Place Buried: Grave Number:	Date of Death:	Place Buried: Grave Number:

Marriage Details

Date of Marriage:	Place of Marriage:	Witness 1:	Witness 2:
Groom's Name:	Age:	Occupation:	Additional Details:
Address:			
Father's Name:	Father's Occupation:		
Mother's Name:	Mother's Occupation:		
Bride's Name:	Age:	Occupation:	
Address:			
Father's Name:	Father's Occupation:		
Mother's Name:	Mother's Occupation:		

Children

Name:	Birth:	Death:	Occupation:	Marriage:	Spouse:	Information:

Census Information

Year:	Address:	Family / Details:	

Great Great Great Grandparents

x3 Great Grandfather		x3 Great Grandmother	
Name:		Name:	
Date of Birth:	Place of Birth:	Date of Birth:	Place of Birth:
Baptised:		Baptised:	
Date of Death:	Place Buried: Grave Number:	Date of Death:	Place Buried: Grave Number:

Marriage Details

Date of Marriage:	Place of Marriage:	Witness 1:	Witness 2:
Groom's Name:	Age:	Occupation:	Additional Details:
Address:			
Father's Name:	Father's Occupation:		
Mother's Name:	Mother's Occupation:		
Bride's Name:	Age:	Occupation:	
Address:			
Father's Name:	Father's Occupation:		
Mother's Name:	Mother's Occupation:		

Children

Name:	Birth:	Death:	Occupation:	Marriage:	Spouse:	Information:

Census Information

Year:	Address:	Family / Details:	

Great Great Great Grandparents

x3 Great Grandfather		x3 Great Grandmother	
Name:		Name:	
Date of Birth:	Place of Birth:	Date of Birth:	Place of Birth:
Baptised:		Baptised:	
Date of Death:	Place Buried: Grave Number:	Date of Death:	Place Buried: Grave Number:

Marriage Details

Date of Marriage:	Place of Marriage:	Witness 1:	Witness 2:
Groom's Name:	Age:	Occupation:	Additional Details:
Address:			
Father's Name:	Father's Occupation:		
Mother's Name:	Mother's Occupation:		
Bride's Name:	Age:	Occupation:	
Address:			
Father's Name:	Father's Occupation:		
Mother's Name:	Mother's Occupation:		

Children

Name:	Birth:	Death:	Occupation:	Marriage:	Spouse:	Information:

Census Information

Year:	Address:	Family / Details:	

Great Great Great Grandparents

x3 Great Grandfather		x3 Great Grandmother	
Name:		Name:	
Date of Birth:	Place of Birth:	Date of Birth:	Place of Birth:
Baptised:		Baptised:	
Date of Death:	Place Buried: Grave Number:	Date of Death:	Place Buried: Grave Number:

Marriage Details

Date of Marriage:	Place of Marriage:	Witness 1:	Witness 2:
Groom's Name:	Age:	Occupation:	Additional Details:
Address:			
Father's Name:	Father's Occupation:		
Mother's Name:	Mother's Occupation:		
Bride's Name:	Age:	Occupation:	
Address:			
Father's Name:	Father's Occupation:		
Mother's Name:	Mother's Occupation:		

Children

Name:	Birth:	Death:	Occupation:	Marriage:	Spouse:	Information:

Census Information

Year:	Address:	Family / Details:	

Mother's Family Tree

Mother's Maiden Name: _____

Mother's Birth Date: _____

Mother's Place of Birth: _____

(see page 16 for more details)

Grandparents – *maternal/mother's side*

Grandfather

Name:		Name:	
Date of Birth:	Place of Birth:	Date of Birth:	Place of Birth:
Baptised:		Baptised:	
Date of Death:	Place Buried: Grave Number:	Date of Death:	Place Buried: Grave Number:

Grandmother

(see above)

Marriage Details

Date of Marriage:	Place of Marriage:	Witness 1:	Witness 2:
Groom's Name:	Age:	Occupation:	Additional Details:
Address:			
Father's Name:	Father's Occupation:		
Mother's Name:	Mother's Occupation:		
Bride's Name:	Age:	Occupation:	
Address:			
Father's Name:	Father's Occupation:		
Mother's Name:	Mother's Occupation:		

Children

Name:	Birth:	Death:	Occupation:	Marriage:	Spouse:	Information:

Census Information

Year:	Address:	Family / Details:	

Great Grandparents

Great Grandfather

Name:			
Date of Birth:	Place of Birth:		
Baptised:			
Date of Death:	Place Buried:		
	Grave Number:		

Great Grandmother

Name:			
Date of Birth:	Place of Birth:		
Baptised:			
Date of Death:	Place Buried:		
	Grave Number:		

Marriage Details

Date of Marriage:	Place of Marriage:	Witness 1:	Witness 2:
Groom's Name:	Age:	Occupation:	Additional Details:
Address:			
Father's Name:	Father's Occupation:		
Mother's Name:	Mother's Occupation:		
Bride's Name:	Age:	Occupation:	
Address:			
Father's Name:	Father's Occupation:		
Mother's Name:	Mother's Occupation:		

Children

Name:	Birth:	Death:	Occupation:	Marriage:	Spouse:	Information:

Census Information

Year:	Address:	Family / Details:	

Great Grandparents

Great Grandfather

Name:			
Date of Birth:	Place of Birth:		
Baptised:			
Date of Death:	Place Buried:		
	Grave Number:		

Great Grandmother

Name:			
Date of Birth:	Place of Birth:		
Baptised:			
Date of Death:	Place Buried:		
	Grave Number:		

Marriage Details

Date of Marriage:	Place of Marriage:	Witness 1:	Witness 2:
Groom's Name:	Age:	Occupation:	Additional Details:
Address:			
Father's Name:	Father's Occupation:		
Mother's Name:	Mother's Occupation:		
Bride's Name:	Age:	Occupation:	
Address:			
Father's Name:	Father's Occupation:		
Mother's Name:	Mother's Occupation:		

Children

Name:	Birth:	Death:	Occupation:	Marriage:	Spouse:	Information:

Census Information

Year:	Address:	Family / Details:	

Great Great Grandparents

x2 Great Grandfather		x2 Great Grandmother	
Name:		Name:	
Date of Birth:	Place of Birth:	Date of Birth:	Place of Birth:
Baptised:		Baptised:	
Date of Death:	Place Buried:	Date of Death:	Place Buried:
	Grave Number:		Grave Number:

Marriage Details

Date of Marriage:	Place of Marriage:	Witness 1:	Witness 2:
Groom's Name:	Age:	Occupation:	Additional Details:
Address:			
Father's Name:	Father's Occupation:		
Mother's Name:	Mother's Occupation:		
Bride's Name:	Age:	Occupation:	
Address:			
Father's Name:	Father's Occupation:		
Mother's Name:	Mother's Occupation:		

Children

Name:	Birth:	Death:	Occupation:	Marriage:	Spouse:	Information:

Census Information

Year:	Address:	Family / Details:	

Great Great Grandparents

x2 Great Grandfather		x2 Great Grandmother	
Name:		Name:	
Date of Birth:	Place of Birth:	Date of Birth:	Place of Birth:
Baptised:		Baptised:	
Date of Death:	Place Buried: Grave Number:	Date of Death:	Place Buried: Grave Number:

Marriage Details

Date of Marriage:	Place of Marriage:	Witness 1:	Witness 2:
Groom's Name:	Age:	Occupation:	Additional Details:
Address:			
Father's Name:	Father's Occupation:		
Mother's Name:	Mother's Occupation:		
Bride's Name:	Age:	Occupation:	
Address:			
Father's Name:	Father's Occupation:		
Mother's Name:	Mother's Occupation:		

Children

Name:	Birth:	Death:	Occupation:	Marriage:	Spouse:	Information:

Census Information

Year:	Address:	Family / Details:	

Great Great Grandparents

x2 Great Grandfather		x2 Great Grandmother	
Name:		Name:	
Date of Birth:	Place of Birth:	Date of Birth:	Place of Birth:
Baptised:		Baptised:	
Date of Death:	Place Buried: Grave Number:	Date of Death:	Place Buried: Grave Number:

Marriage Details

Date of Marriage:	Place of Marriage:	Witness 1:	Witness 2:
Groom's Name:	Age:	Occupation:	Additional Details:
Address:			
Father's Name:	Father's Occupation:		
Mother's Name:	Mother's Occupation:		
Bride's Name:	Age:	Occupation:	
Address:			
Father's Name:	Father's Occupation:		
Mother's Name:	Mother's Occupation:		

Children

Name:	Birth:	Death:	Occupation:	Marriage:	Spouse:	Information:

Census Information

Year:	Address:	Family / Details:	

Great Great Grandparents

x2 Great Grandfather		x2 Great Grandmother	
Name:		Name:	
Date of Birth:	Place of Birth:	Date of Birth:	Place of Birth:
Baptised:		Baptised:	
Date of Death:	Place Buried: Grave Number:	Date of Death:	Place Buried: Grave Number:

Marriage Details

Date of Marriage:	Place of Marriage:	Witness 1:	Witness 2:
Groom's Name:	Age:	Occupation:	Additional Details:
Address:			
Father's Name:	Father's Occupation:		
Mother's Name:	Mother's Occupation:		
Bride's Name:	Age:	Occupation:	
Address:			
Father's Name:	Father's Occupation:		
Mother's Name:	Mother's Occupation:		

Children

Name:	Birth:	Death:	Occupation:	Marriage:	Spouse:	Information:

Census Information

Year:	Address:	Family / Details:	

Great Great Great Grandparents

x3 Great Grandfather		x3 Great Grandmother	
Name:		Name:	
Date of Birth:	Place of Birth:	Date of Birth:	Place of Birth:
Baptised:		Baptised:	
Date of Death:	Place Buried: Grave Number:	Date of Death:	Place Buried: Grave Number:

Marriage Details

Date of Marriage:	Place of Marriage:	Witness 1:	Witness 2:
Groom's Name:	Age:	Occupation:	Additional Details:
Address:			
Father's Name:	Father's Occupation:		
Mother's Name:	Mother's Occupation:		
Bride's Name:	Age:	Occupation:	
Address:			
Father's Name:	Father's Occupation:		
Mother's Name:	Mother's Occupation:		

Children

Name:	Birth:	Death:	Occupation:	Marriage:	Spouse:	Information:

Census Information

Year:	Address:	Family / Details:	

Great Great Great Grandparents

x3 Great Grandfather		x3 Great Grandmother	
Name:		Name:	
Date of Birth:	Place of Birth:	Date of Birth:	Place of Birth:
Baptised:		Baptised:	
Date of Death:	Place Buried: Grave Number:	Date of Death:	Place Buried: Grave Number:

Marriage Details

Date of Marriage:	Place of Marriage:	Witness 1:	Witness 2:
Groom's Name:	Age:	Occupation:	Additional Details:
Address:			
Father's Name:	Father's Occupation:		
Mother's Name:	Mother's Occupation:		
Bride's Name:	Age:	Occupation:	
Address:			
Father's Name:	Father's Occupation:		
Mother's Name:	Mother's Occupation:		

Children

Name:	Birth:	Death:	Occupation:	Marriage:	Spouse:	Information:

Census Information

Year:	Address:	Family / Details:	

Great Great Great Grandparents

x3 Great Grandfather		x3 Great Grandmother	
Name:		Name:	
Date of Birth:	Place of Birth:	Date of Birth:	Place of Birth:
Baptised:		Baptised:	
Date of Death:	Place Buried:	Date of Death:	Place Buried:
	Grave Number:		Grave Number:

Marriage Details

Date of Marriage:	Place of Marriage:	Witness 1:	Witness 2:
Groom's Name:	Age:	Occupation:	Additional Details:
Address:			
Father's Name:	Father's Occupation:		
Mother's Name:	Mother's Occupation:		
Bride's Name:	Age:	Occupation:	
Address:			
Father's Name:	Father's Occupation:		
Mother's Name:	Mother's Occupation:		

Children

Name:	Birth:	Death:	Occupation:	Marriage:	Spouse:	Information:

Census Information

Year:	Address:	Family / Details:	

Great Great Great Grandparents

x3 Great Grandfather		x3 Great Grandmother	
Name:		Name:	
Date of Birth:	Place of Birth:	Date of Birth:	Place of Birth:
Baptised:		Baptised:	
Date of Death:	Place Buried:	Date of Death:	Place Buried:
	Grave Number:		Grave Number:

Marriage Details

Date of Marriage:	Place of Marriage:	Witness 1:	Witness 2:
Groom's Name:	Age:	Occupation:	Additional Details:
Address:			
Father's Name:	Father's Occupation:		
Mother's Name:	Mother's Occupation:		
Bride's Name:	Age:	Occupation:	
Address:			
Father's Name:	Father's Occupation:		
Mother's Name:	Mother's Occupation:		

Children

Name:	Birth:	Death:	Occupation:	Marriage:	Spouse:	Information:

Census Information

Year:	Address:	Family / Details:	

Great Great Great Grandparents

x3 Great Grandfather		x3 Great Grandmother	
Name:		Name:	
Date of Birth:	Place of Birth:	Date of Birth:	Place of Birth:
Baptised:		Baptised:	
Date of Death:	Place Buried: Grave Number:	Date of Death:	Place Buried: Grave Number:

Marriage Details

Date of Marriage:	Place of Marriage:	Witness 1:	Witness 2:
Groom's Name:	Age:	Occupation:	Additional Details:
Address:			
Father's Name:	Father's Occupation:		
Mother's Name:	Mother's Occupation:		
Bride's Name:	Age:	Occupation:	
Address:			
Father's Name:	Father's Occupation:		
Mother's Name:	Mother's Occupation:		

Children

Name:	Birth:	Death:	Occupation:	Marriage:	Spouse:	Information:

Census Information

Year:	Address:	Family / Details:	

Great Great Great Grandparents

x3 Great Grandfather		x3 Great Grandmother	
Name:		Name:	
Date of Birth:	Place of Birth:	Date of Birth:	Place of Birth:
Baptised:		Baptised:	
Date of Death:	Place Buried: Grave Number:	Date of Death:	Place Buried: Grave Number:

Marriage Details

Date of Marriage:	Place of Marriage:	Witness 1:	Witness 2:
Groom's Name:	Age:	Occupation:	Additional Details:
Address:			
Father's Name:	Father's Occupation:		
Mother's Name:	Mother's Occupation:		
Bride's Name:	Age:	Occupation:	
Address:			
Father's Name:	Father's Occupation:		
Mother's Name:	Mother's Occupation:		

Children

Name:	Birth:	Death:	Occupation:	Marriage:	Spouse:	Information:

Census Information

Year:	Address:	Family / Details:	

Great Great Great Grandparents

x3 Great Grandfather		x3 Great Grandmother	
Name:		Name:	
Date of Birth:	Place of Birth:	Date of Birth:	Place of Birth:
Baptised:		Baptised:	
Date of Death:	Place Buried:	Date of Death:	Place Buried:
	Grave Number:		Grave Number:

Marriage Details

Date of Marriage:	Place of Marriage:	Witness 1:	Witness 2:
Groom's Name:	Age:	Occupation:	Additional Details:
Address:			
Father's Name:	Father's Occupation:		
Mother's Name:	Mother's Occupation:		
Bride's Name:	Age:	Occupation:	
Address:			
Father's Name:	Father's Occupation:		
Mother's Name:	Mother's Occupation:		

Children

Name:	Birth:	Death:	Occupation:	Marriage:	Spouse:	Information:

Census Information

Year:	Address:	Family / Details:	

Great Great Great Grandparents

x3 Great Grandfather		x3 Great Grandmother	
Name:		Name:	
Date of Birth:	Place of Birth:	Date of Birth:	Place of Birth:
Baptised:		Baptised:	
Date of Death:	Place Buried: Grave Number:	Date of Death:	Place Buried: Grave Number:

Marriage Details

Date of Marriage:	Place of Marriage:	Witness 1:	Witness 2:
Groom's Name:	Age:	Occupation:	Additional Details:
Address:			
Father's Name:	Father's Occupation:		
Mother's Name:	Mother's Occupation:		
Bride's Name:	Age:	Occupation:	
Address:			
Father's Name:	Father's Occupation:		
Mother's Name:	Mother's Occupation:		

Children

Name:	Birth:	Death:	Occupation:	Marriage:	Spouse:	Information:

Census Information

Year:	Address:	Family / Details:	

Certificates Log

It is useful to note down certificates as you acquire them. List names going back in time i.e. parents, grandparents, great grandparents and so on, leaving a space/spaces for those you have not yet found or named.

Simply name your ancestor, add their relationship to you and then tick the box of which certificate you have acquired.

Name	Relationship	Birth	Death	Marriage	Other

Name	Relationship	Birth	Death	Marriage	Other

Name	Relationship	Birth	Death	Marriage	Other

Name	Relationship	Birth	Death	Marriage	Other

Ancestors Military Information

Name	Birth Date	Rank	Theatre (Conflict)	Information

Female Ancestors in World War I & II

During World Wars One and Two women performed vital work, serving the country in roles that had previously been closed off to them. During your research you may have discovered the work some of your female ancestors may have done, through services such as the Women's Royal Navy Service, the Women's Voluntary Service or through factory work or professional roles that women had previously been discouraged or barred from. Use this table to list the roles your female ancestors performed.

Name:	Role:	Other Information:

Ancestors Who Emigrated

Name	Departure Date	Ship Name	Information	Return Date *(if applicable)*

Ancestors Grave Information

Name	Burial Place	Plot Number	Grave Inscription

Family stories and legends to uncover

Photographs

Name/s:	Date:	Location:

Name/s:	Date:	Location:

Name/s:	Date:	Location:

Name/s:	Date:	Location:

Name/s:	Date:	Location:

Name/s:	Date:	Location:

Name/s:	Date:	Location:

Additional Children

It was commonplace in centuries past for families to have many children – it was not unusual to have over 15 children per family. Because of this, here are some additional tables for you to log any further births that may not have fit in the previous logs. You may have also found, through your research, that a parent may have died and their widowed spouse subsequently remarried and had more children, in which case you may wish to log those details too, or the issues of a parents' previous marriage.

Parents:						
Name:	Birth:	Death:	Occupation:	Marriage:	Spouse:	Information:

Parents:						
Name:	Birth:	Death:	Occupation:	Marriage:	Spouse:	Information:

Parents:						
Name:	Birth:	Death:	Occupation:	Marriage:	Spouse:	Information:

Additional Family Trees

Perhaps there is a great uncle or cousin whose family or issue (children) you would like to look into, or maybe you have managed to track your lineage back over six generations and want to research even further. If so, here are a selection of additional family trees you can use, including some landscape options overleaf.

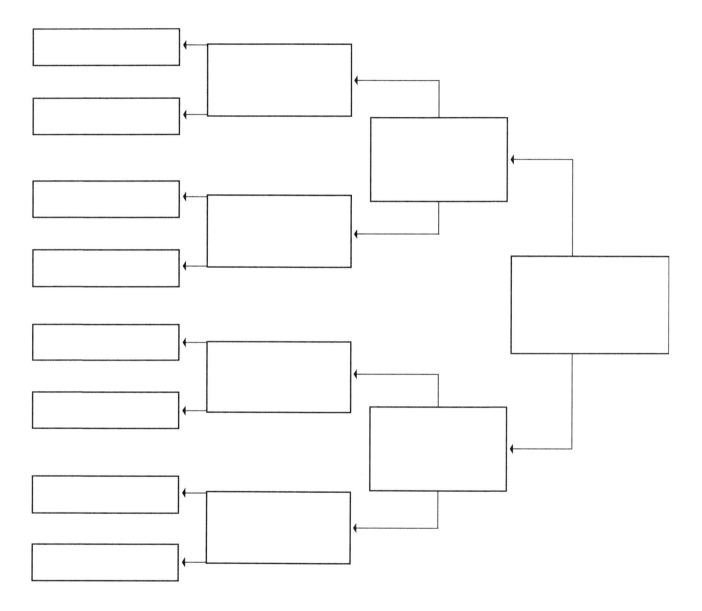

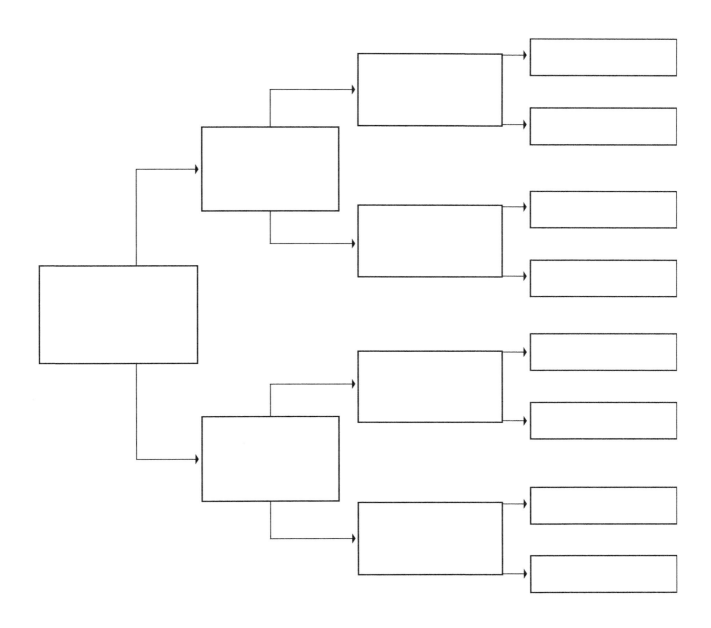

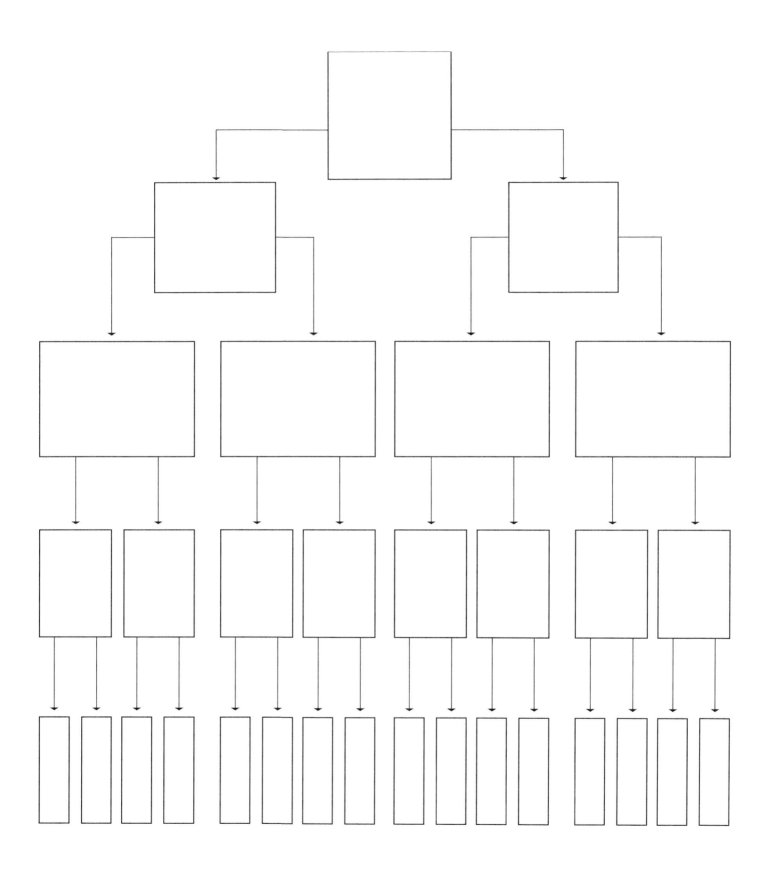

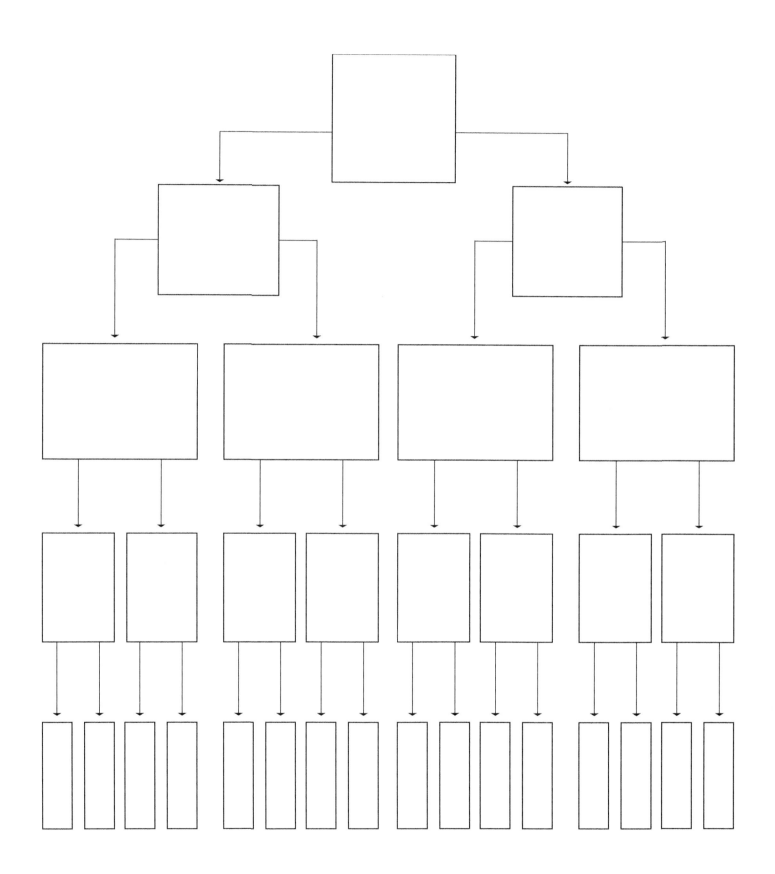

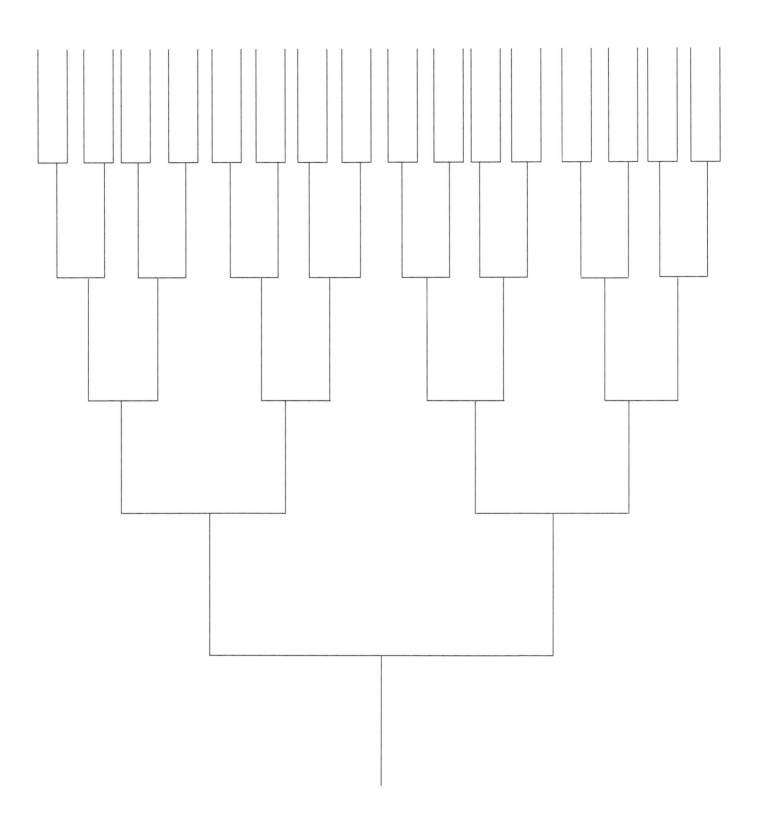

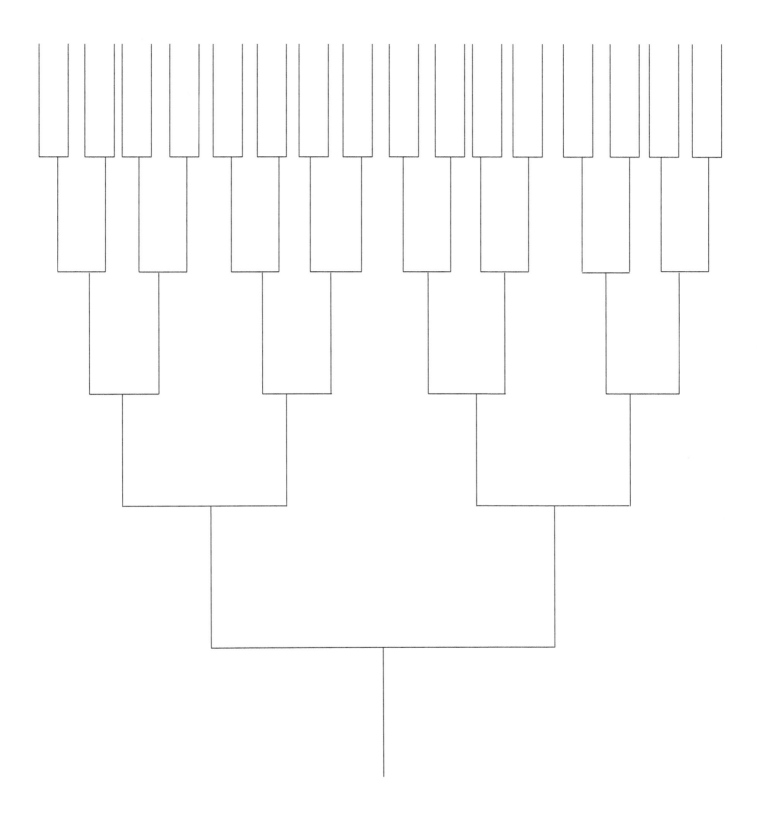

Helpful Websites

The following are a selection of websites that you may find helpful during your research; these include archival websites as well as search engines.

Website	URL	Description
Free UK Genealogy	www.freeukgenealogy.org.uk	Free search of UK births, deaths, marriage, census and parish records
National Archives	www.nationalarchives.gov.uk	UK's national archives, including military records
Family Records	www.familyrecords.gov.uk	The UK Government's general registry office and certificate ordering service
Free Family Tree Templates	www.freefamilytreetemplates.com	Free family tree templates
Search For Ancestors	www.searchforancestors.com	A database of genealogical search engines
Ancestry	www.ancestry.com	Family/ancestry database with access to census records, passenger lists, DNA tests and more
Find My Past	www.findmypast.com	British, American and Canadian database
Family Search	www.familysearch.org	Ancestral database
My Heritage	www.myheritage.com	Ancestral database
Roots Web	www.home.rootsweb.com	Ancestral database
The British Newspaper Archive	www.britishnewspaperarchive.co.uk	Hundreds of historic newspapers from Britain and Ireland
Commonwealth War Graves Commission	www.cwgc.org	War graves locators, war diaries records and more
Find A Grave	www.findagrave.com	Global database of cemeteries and memorials
Billion Graves	www.billiongraves.com	Database of graves
Find A Church	www.findachurch.co.uk	UK directory of churches including photographs and maps
Forces War Records	www.forces-war-records.co.uk	Millions of servicemen's records
Scotland's People	www.scotlandspeople.gov.uk	Official records for Scotland
Cyndi's List	www.cyndislist.com	A genealogy blog listing other places to search
Family History Daily	www.familyhistorydaily.com	Tips and advice for researching your family tree
Afri Geneas	www.afrigeneas.com	Dedicated to researching African heritage particular to the Americas
Jewish Gen	www.jewishgen.org	Global database for Jewish ancestry
Family Tree Magazine	www.familytreemagazine.com	Articles and tools to assist your research
We Relate	www.werelate.org	A free public-service Wiki run by volunteers
Society of Genealogist	www.sog.org.uk	Family history centre

URLs correct at time of publication. User discretion advised. Websites may have changed ownership or content since publication of this book.

Notes

Notes

Notes

Notes

Notes

Notes

Notes

Notes

Research Log

The process of tracking down your ancestry involves a lot of research from various sources. Throughout your research you will come across useful information and URLs. However, it is very easy to forget where you saw certain details and misplace references. This is a simple log enabling you to note what information you have found and where you found it. Information may include vital historical documents or simply a webpage detailing various occupations from certain time periods.

Date	Search Details	URL/Source	Notes

Date	Search Details	URL/Source	Notes

Date	Search Details	URL/Source	Notes

Thank you

Thank you for buying the Genealogy Journal

Please let us know what you think of this book by leaving a review on Amazon.
Leave suggestions or requests for any future books or editions too.

Other titles by Quinthos Publishing, available on Amazon:

Progress Journal
This journal has been created to help you nurture your wellbeing through introspection and mindfulness. As well as monthly diary entries, with room for notes, to-do lists, prospective goals and habit-trackers, there are themed progress questions exploring your proudest moments, greatest fears, inspirations and ideas. Monthly quotes motivate you as you journey through the book, interspersed with puzzles to occupy and entertain you. Search 'Progress Journal Quinthos Publishing' on Amazon to find an assortment of cover colours and styles to choose from.

The Masterplan
Filled with a year's worth of daily diary entries, this undated planner also includes checklists, habit trackers, a year at a glance, goals and ambitions planners and more. Search 'The Masterplan Quinthos Publishing' on Amazon to find a selection of beautifully designed covers to choose from.

Quinthos Quizbook
An assortment of puzzles, brainteasers, quizzes and trivia, exploring history, geography, science, popular culture and medicine, as well as visual challenges and word-based games. If you enjoy Word Searches, Logic Squares, Word Worms, Pop Quizzes and Word Wheels, this is for you, along with many more puzzles. Whether a travel accompaniment, mental health break or rainy day activity, the Quinthos Quizbook is filled with fun and varied puzzles and questions for all levels.

Printed in Great Britain
by Amazon